I didn't know that

the Sun is a star

© Aladdin Books Ltd 1997

Produced by

Aladdin Books Ltd

28 Percy Street

London W1P 0LD

First published in the United States in 1997 by

Copper Beech Books,

an imprint of

The Millbrook Press

2 Old New Milford Road

Brookfield, Connecticut 06804

Concept, editorial, and design by

David West Children's Books

Designer: David West

Illustrators: Francis Phillips, Ian Thompson, Rob Shone, Jo Moore

Library of Congress Cataloging-in-Publication Data
Petty, Kate.
The sun is a star and other amazing facts about space / by Kate Petty ;
illustrated by Francis Phillips and Ian Thompson.
p. cm. — (I didn't know that—)
Includes index.
Summary: Provides information about stars, the sun and the planets, comets,
and other astronomical phenomena.
ISBN 0-7613-0593-9 (trade hc). — ISBN 0-7613-0567-X (s&l)
1. Astronomy—Juvenile literature. [1. Astronomy.] I. Phillips, Francis, ill.
II. Thompson, Ian, 1964- ill. III. Title. IV. Series.
QB46.P5 1997   96-43328
523—dc20   CIP AC

I didn't know that

the Sun

is a star

Kate Petty

COPPER BEECH BOOKS
BROOKFIELD, CONNECTICUT

I didn't know that

Introduction

Did *you* know that Saturn is so light it could float in water?

... that the sky on Venus is orange?

... that there might be life on one of Jupiter's moons?

Discover for yourself amazing facts about our solar system and from the incredible depths of the universe beyond it.

Watch for this symbol that means there is a fun project for you to try.

Is it true or is it false? Watch for this symbol and try to answer the question before reading on for the answer.

I didn't know that

stars are born in clouds – vast, collapsing clouds of hydrogen gas and dust, millions of miles away in outer space. As the gas and dust are drawn in they get hotter and hotter and clump together as a new star.

nebula   star starts to form   star shines

After about 50 million years the inside of a new star becomes hot enough to make it shine.

The correct name for a star cloud is *nebula* (plural: nebulae), which is simply what the ancient Romans called a cloud.

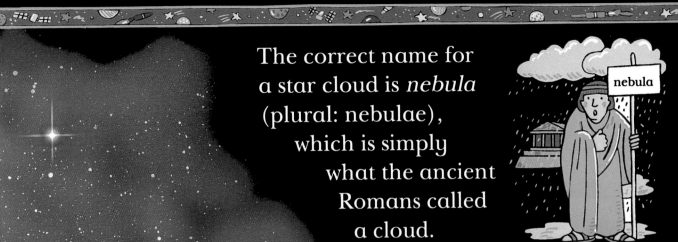

True or false?
You can see a horse's head among the stars.

Answer: **True**
There is a famous dark nebula called the Horse's Head. It got its name because it looks like one!

I didn't know that

the sun is a star. Our sun is a very ordinary bright star, even though it's a million times bigger than the Earth. It is almost half way through its 10 billion-year life.

WARNING
NEVER LOOK DIRECTLY AT THE SUN.

The heat at the sun's surface is 10,000° F – cool compared with the center, where it is at least 27,000,000° F!

10,000°F

27,000,000°F

Prominence

Cutaway of the sun

If you could drive to the sun in your family's car, it would take 150 years.

True or false?

The sun has a spotty face.

 SEARCH & FIND Can you find the planet Earth? FIND & SEARCH

Answer: **True**

Sunspots look like dark freckles on the sun's face. Some sunspots are as big as 120,000 miles across.

Many people in history have worshiped the sun. The Aztecs offered human hearts to their sun god, Huitzilopochtli, to give him strength in his nightly battles with the forces of darkness.

I didn't know that

there are *red giants* and *white dwarfs* in space. When a star is about to die it swells up into a red giant. Normally the outer layers puff away, leaving a burning core, or white dwarf. This cools into a *black dwarf*.

Red giant

Really massive stars have shorter lives. When they reach their red giant stage, they are called *supergiants*.

Supergiant

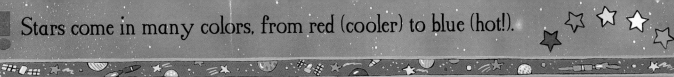

Stars come in many colors, from red (cooler) to blue (hot!).

Supernova

Alternatively a massive star might end its life in a spectacular explosion, called a *supernova*. It can blow up so completely that it leaves no core at all.

White dwarf

 True or false?
You can hear the explosion of a supernova in space.

Answer: **False**
You can't hear anything in space, even though the explosion of a supernova is like millions of atomic bombs going off.

SEARCH & FIND Can you find the black dwarf? FIND SEARCH &

11

Mercury   Venus   Mars   Jupiter   Saturn   Uranus   Neptune   Pluto

The Romans named the five planets they could see after their gods. Astronomers kept up the tradition when they discovered the other three.

KEY

Sun

Mercury

Venus

Earth

Mars

Asteroid belt

Jupiter

Saturn

Uranus

Neptune

Pluto

Until about 500 years ago people believed that the Earth was the center of the universe. Any other theory was thought shocking.

Early astronomers' drawings would show Earth at the center of the universe.

True or false?

Pluto is the farthest planet from the sun.

Answer: **True and false**
Pluto's orbit is tilted, making Neptune slightly farther from the sun, sometimes!

I didn't know that the planets go around the sun. Nine planets and a band of *asteroids* go around the sun. The pull of the sun's *gravity* holds them in *orbit*. The planets shine in the light from the sun.

The first four planets are rocky, the second four, gassy and the ninth, rocky.

I didn't know that

a day on Venus is longer than a year. A planet's year is the time it takes to orbit the sun. A planet's day is the time it takes to spin on its axis. As Venus takes 225 days to orbit the sun and 243 days to spin on its axis, a Venusian day is longer than its year!

Mercury

Venus

Mercury is the planet closest to the sun. It is small and very hot. It is rocky like our moon, and about one-third bigger.

14

True or false?
If you visited Venus you would be crushed flat by the *atmosphere*.

Answer: **True**

The Venusian atmosphere is made up of dense gases, which are very heavy. The Venera *space probes* were crushed soon after landing.

SEARCH & FIND
Can you find the Venera probe?
FIND & SEARCH

Find out where to look for Venus. It is easy to spot in the evening or morning sky. Mercury can only be seen just before sunrise or just after sunset.

I didn't know that

there are no Martians on Mars. Mars is too cold and dry and the air is too thin for there to be life today. But scientists now think that maybe water once flowed on Mars and that millions of years ago there might have been microscopic bacteria-like creatures there.

H.G.Wells wrote about a Martian invasion in his famous book called *War of the Worlds,* in 1898. All the Martians were destroyed by bacteria.

Mars's huge volcano, Olympus Mons, has a base bigger than California!

The ice caps on Mars shrink in the summer as the ice melts.

There are ice caps at the North and South Poles on Mars. The South Pole is frozen carbon dioxide but at the North Pole it's probably water ice.

SEARCH & FIND
Can you find the space probe?
FIND & SEARCH

True or false?
Mars is red because it is rusty.

Answer: **True**
Space probes have sampled the soil on Mars and found that it contains iron oxide – or rust. Photos show that the rocky surface is red and the sky pink.

SEARCH & FIND & FIND & SEARCH &

Can you find Jupiter's 16 moons?

Io

Jupiter has four big moons – Callisto, Europa, Ganymede, and Io – and twelve smaller ones.

Ganymede

True or false?
The Great Red Spot on Jupiter is a raging storm.

Answer: **True**
Astronomers have wondered about the Red Spot for hundreds of years. Recent pictures from space probes show that it is a tornado in Jupiter's clouds, bigger than Earth.

Callisto

I didn't know that

Jupiter is made of gas. No spacecraft will ever land on the giant planet Jupiter because there are no solid surfaces to land on. The outside is all swirling gases and the inside is —— a sea of liquid hydrogen.

Europa

Arthur C. Clarke's story *2001: A Space Odyssey* mentions Europa. In fact there is a tiny chance that there might be life beneath Europa's icy oceans.

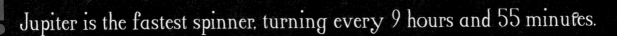

Jupiter is the fastest spinner, turning every 9 hours and 55 minutes.

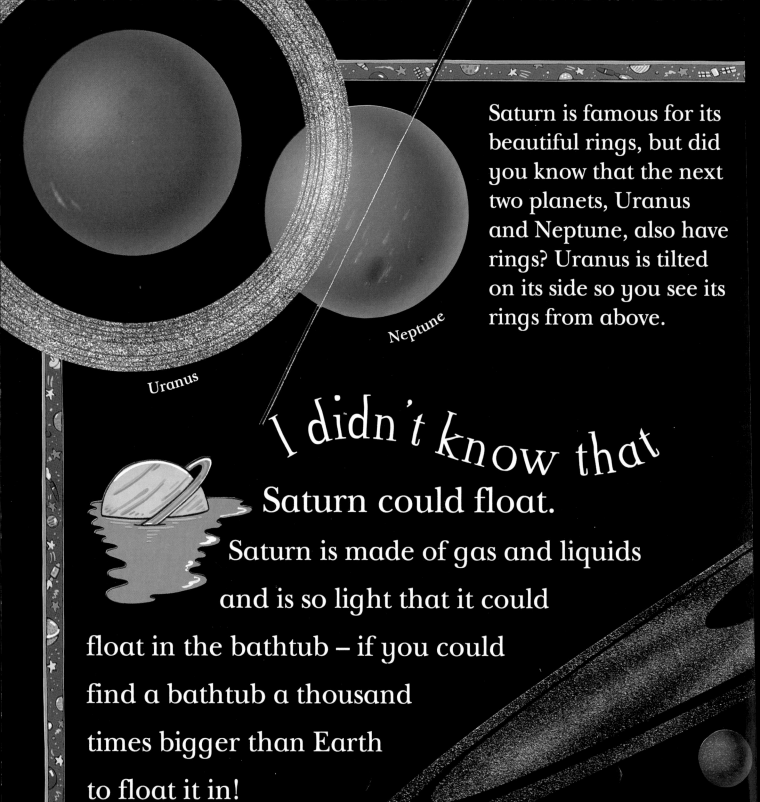

Saturn is famous for its beautiful rings, but did you know that the next two planets, Uranus and Neptune, also have rings? Uranus is tilted on its side so you see its rings from above.

Neptune

Uranus

I didn't know that

Saturn could float. Saturn is made of gas and liquids and is so light that it could float in the bathtub – if you could find a bathtub a thousand times bigger than Earth to float it in!

Saturn

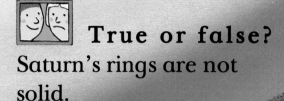

True or false?
Saturn's rings are not solid.

Saturn's rings are made up of ice and dust particles.

Answer: **False**
Saturn's three main rings are in fact thousands of bands of ice-covered rocks, ranging in size from stones to boulders.

Pluto

The most distant planet – Pluto – may not be a planet at all. It is smaller than our moon and made of rock.

Saturn has at least 18 moons, the most of any planet.

I didn't know that

meteorites are pieces of old planets. A meteorite is any piece of rock or metal from outer space – from a few ounces to several thousand tons – that survives the fall to Earth. Scientists can tell whether a meteorite has come from an asteroid or the moon or even from Mars.

This crater in Arizona was made by a massive iron meteorite nearly fifty thousand years ago. It must have vaporized on impact, because there is almost nothing there.

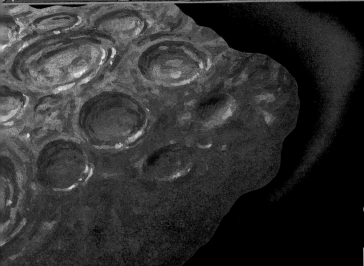

 True or false?
A meteorite might have dramatically changed the course of history.

 Meteors are what we call shooting stars. They are pieces of space dust, from the tail of a comet, burning up as they enter the atmosphere. Watch out for them – especially around mid-August

Answer: **True**
The 26,000 meteorites that land every year cause very little damage. But many scientists believe that a huge meteorite crashed into the Earth 65 million years ago, altering the climate and causing the dinosaurs to die out.

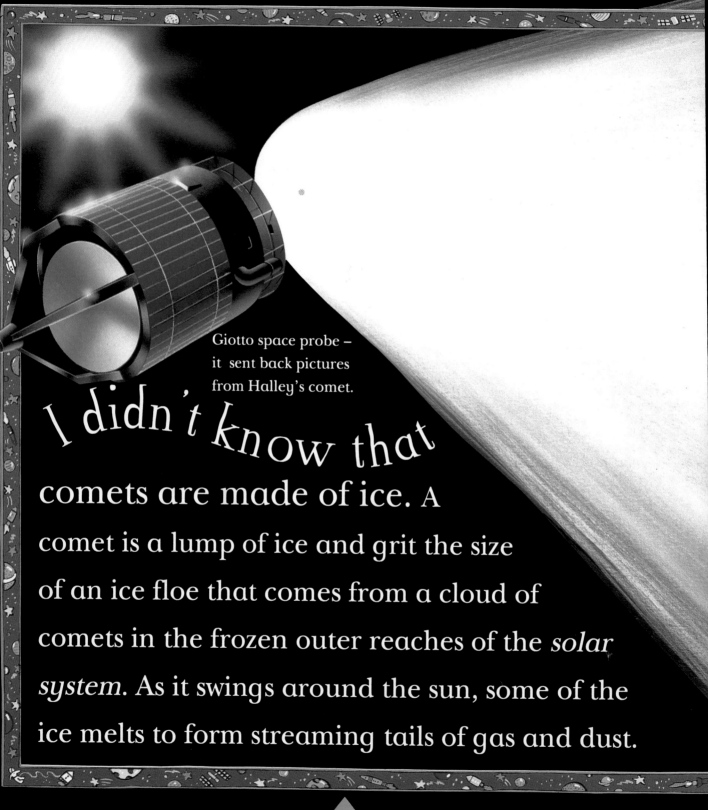

A comet's gas tail always points away from the sun.

Giotto space probe – it sent back pictures from Halley's comet.

I didn't know that

comets are made of ice. A comet is a lump of ice and grit the size of an ice floe that comes from a cloud of comets in the frozen outer reaches of the *solar system*. As it swings around the sun, some of the ice melts to form streaming tails of gas and dust.

Can you find the comet's core?

True or false?
A comet could not possibly crash into a planet.

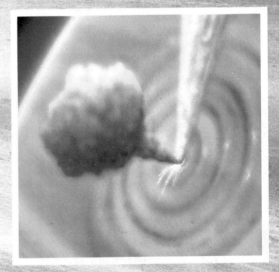

Halley's Comet appears in our skies every 76 years. When it appeared in 1066, the English blamed it for their defeat in the Battle of Hastings. You can see the comet in the Bayeux Tapestry, which tells the story of the battle.

Answer: **False**
In 1994 a comet smashed into Jupiter. It was called Shoemaker-Levy 9 after the people who first saw it. Spectacular photographs of the impact made the front page of every newspaper.

The Bayeux Tapestry shows Halley's Comet, top center.

The star in the Christmas story might have been a comet.

I didn't know that

I live in the Milky Way.

Our sun is just one of the 100 billion stars that make up the Milky Way *galaxy*. We live out on one of the spiraling arms, 28,000 *light years* away from the center.

SEARCH & FIND
Can you find where you live?
X
FIND & SEARCH

1

2

3

There are four different shapes of galaxy: 1. irregular, 2. ellipse (egg-shaped), 3. barred spiral, and spiral. Our Milky Way is a spiral galaxy.

Milky Way

On a clear night you can sometimes see a misty band across the sky. This is the millions of shining stars in one of the arms of the Milky Way galaxy.

27

I didn't know that

there are holes in space.

The bigger the star, the greater is the pull of its gravity. When a really massive star collapses, it pulls everything in on itself. Nothing can escape, not even

light. So the star becomes a *black hole*. It's there but there is nothing to see.

Albert Einstein (1879-1955) was a famous physicist who figured out that there must be black holes, long before anyone was able to prove that they existed.

28

Sometimes pairs of stars go around each other. If one is much brighter than the other, it looks from the Earth as if a single star is flashing on and off as one spins in front of the other.

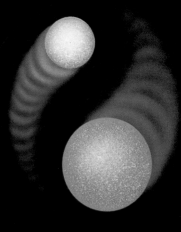

After a supernova explosion, most of the star is blown away. A core may be left, called a *neutron star*. When it spins, it sends out radio waves and is known as a pulsar. When astronomers first picked up these signals they thought they were from aliens.

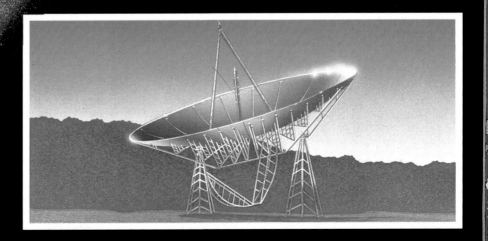

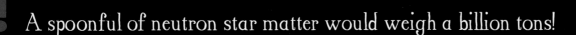
A spoonful of neutron star matter would weigh a billion tons!

Glossary

Asteroid
A piece of rock or metal that orbits the sun, usually as part of the asteroid belt.

Atmosphere
The protective layer of gases around a planet.

Black dwarf
The cinder left when a white dwarf has burned out.

Black hole
A collapsed star that has such strong gravity that nothing can escape from it.

Galaxy
A collection of millions of stars.

Gravity
The natural pull of one object on another.

Light year
5.88 trillion miles – the distance traveled by a ray of light in one year.

Meteor
A shooting star made by dust from space burning up as it enters the atmosphere.

Meteorite
A piece of rock from space that has landed on Earth.

Nebula
The cloud of gas and dust in space from which a star is formed.

Neutron star
The core of a supernova that sometimes remains after it has exploded.

Orbit
The path taken by an object circling a star or planet in space.

Prominence
Glowing gas from the surface of the sun that looks like giant flames.

Red giant
A stage in the life of a star when it nears the end of its life and swells up.

Solar system
Our sun and everything that orbits it.

Space probe
An unmanned spacecraft that sends back information from its explorations in space.

Sunspots
Dark spots on the surface of the sun.

Supergiant
A huge star that has quickly become a "red giant."

Supernova
The explosion at the end of the life of a massive star.

White dwarf
One of the final stages in the life of a star when it becomes a white-hot ember.

Index